Flags

By
Maureen Dockendorf
and Sharon Jeroski

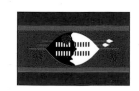

Series Literacy Consultant
Dr Ros Fisher

Pearson Education Limited
Edinburgh Gate
Harlow
Essex CM20 2JE
England

www.longman.co.uk

ISBN 0 582 84121 6

Colour reproduction by Colourscan, Singapore
Printed and bound in China by Leo Paper Products Ltd.

The Publisher's policy Is to use paper manufactured from sustainable forests.

10 9 8 7 6 5 4 3

The following people from **DK** have
contributed to the development of this product:
Art Director Rachael Foster

Martin Wilson **Managing Art Editor**	**Managing Editor** Marie Greenwood
Sarah Crouch **Design**	**Editorial** Hannah Wilson
Helen McFarland **Picture Research**	**Production** Gordana Simakovic
Richard Czapnik, Andy Smith **Cover Design**	**DTP** David McDonald

Consultants Philip Wilkinson

Dorling Kindersley would like to thank: Rose Horridge in the DK Picture Library; Ed Merrit and Simon Mumford for cartography;
and Johnny Pau for additional cover design work.

Picture Credits: Alamy Images: Steve Allen 1c; Jan Baks 13br; Chris Bellentine 4tl; Michael Grant 18tl; Chris Jackson 4cla; Bragi Thor
Josefsson/Nordicphotos.com 27cl; Pictor International/Imagestate 4b, 8bl; Popperfoto 29c. Associated Press AP: Stringer 15tr, 28bc. Bridgeman Art
Library, London/New York: Bibliothèque Nationale, Paris 6tr. © The British Museum: 5t. Corbis: 19t, 28cr; Dean Conger 18b; Historical Picture
Archive 20bl; Michale S. Lewis 28bl; Galen Rowell 8cr, 28tr; Pascal Le Segretain /SYGMA 7tr; Wendy Stone 29cl; Michael S. Yamashita 9cr.
Mary Evans Picture Library: Explorer/ADPC 11b. Werner Forman Archive: Museum für Vülkerkunde, Basel 17tr. Getty Images: Doug Armand
24br;Tony Feder/Allsport 22cr. NASA: Jacques Descloitres, MODIS Rapid Response Team, NASA/GSFC 14bl. Pa Photos: EPA 29br.
Cover: Alamy Images: Brian Lawrence/Imagestate front t. Getty Images: Tony Feder/Allsport back.

All other images: DK Dorling Kindersley © 2004. For further information see www.dkimages.com
Dorling Kindersley Ltd., 80 Strand, London WC2R ORL

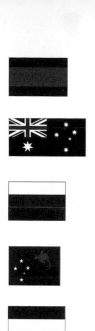

Contents

Flags Are Flying   4

Flags of Many Colours   8

Symbols on Flags   13

Changing Flags   20

International Flags   24

Flag Customs and Traditions   27

Flags of the World   30

Index   32

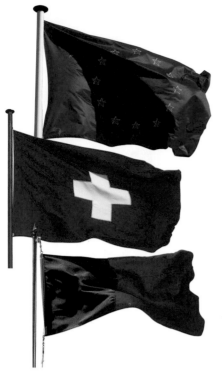

Flags Are Flying

A flag is a cloth attached to a rope or pole and is a signal or symbol. It identifies a nation. It is an important symbol, representing the beliefs, hopes and dreams of the people who wave it. A flag is used to rally people to a common cause. A flag sometimes tells a story. Colours, patterns and designs make each country's flag different.

Flags are made to be seen.

Each flag is unique for every country.

Ancient Flags

No one knows exactly what the first flag looked like or who used it. Many early people used flags to identify themselves and to signal from a distance.

In ancient Egypt warriors carried fans and carvings high on poles to show their identity. Ancient Roman soldiers carried objects, often with small pieces of cloth attached, which identified their army units. In China and India flags represented rulers or kings. In some cultures, if a flag fell in battle, it meant that the leader had been killed.

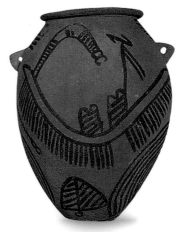

This ancient Egyptian pot shows a very early form of a flag on the top right.

These carved symbols were carried on poles and were early forms of flags.

This is a modern reconstruction of an ancient Roman flag.

Flags of the Middle Ages

In the Middle Ages cities, countries and powerful people used flags to identify themselves. Crosses, crescents, trefoils (symbols based on flowers or herbs with three leaves), lions, falcons, unicorns and dragons were sewn onto coloured fabric. These images were symbols that displayed information about the people who carried them. In battle, soldiers could recognize friends and enemies from a distance. If a city was captured, then a flag was raised over its walls to show who was the new ruler.

This artwork shows a battle scene from the Hundred Years' War between France and England, which began in 1337.

Pennants and Pennons

Flags come in many shapes, each with a special name. There are rectangular, triangular and square flags. A few have tails or fringes. Pennants are long, narrow flags. They are usually triangular. Pennons are also long and thin, but they often divide into two at the end.

British army pennons were hung from lances.

This old Chinese pennant flew on boats.

Flags of Different Nations

Today most of the world is divided into nations, and all nations have their own flags. Some of these flags were designed hundreds of years ago. Others were designed recently. All the flags represent ideas or values that are important to that nation.

National flags are waved proudly at international gatherings to identify countries.

Many flags reflect their nation's past. They contain colours or patterns that represent significant events in a nation's history. Others reflect the geography of a nation, its natural features and its people. Some flags display symbols that represent the beliefs, customs and culture, or way of life, of the people.

National Flag Shapes

Kuwait

Nepal

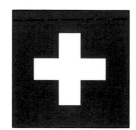

Switzerland

Most modern national flags are rectangular, like Kuwait's flag. Nepal's flag is unusual because it is made of two joined triangles. Switzerland's flag is different from most flags because it is square.

Flags of Many Colours

National flags come in a rainbow of colours that are bold and easy to see from a distance. They are usually arranged in simple patterns that help people recognize the flag instantly. The colours represent things that are important to the people of each nation.

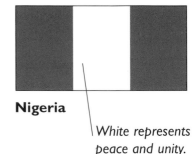

Nigeria

White represents peace and unity.

Colours of Nature

Green often symbolizes nature. Nigeria's flag is green and white. A student called Michael Taiwo Akinkunmi designed this flag to represent the fields and forests of his country. In 1958 his flag was chosen from almost 3,000 entries in a competition.

Brazil also has a flag with green on it. This represents the lush rainforests that cover most of the country. Yellow or gold represents many things. Ukraine's flag has a yellow stripe that represents wheat fields.

Brazil is home to the Amazon rainforest.

Brazil

A yellow diamond represents Brazil's mineral resources.

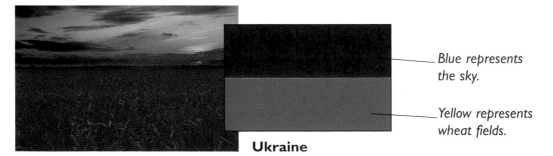

Blue represents the sky.

Yellow represents wheat fields.

Ukraine

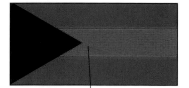

Many island countries, such as the Bahamas, have blue on their flags to represent the sea that surrounds them. Other countries use blue to represent the sky, and some see blue as a colour of peace.

Red often symbolises blood, or the sacrifice people made to fight for their country's independence. Red is also used to represent a number of different political or religious beliefs.

White sometimes represents ice or snow like Finland's flag. However, white also stands for hope, love, freedom or peace.

The five colours in the flag of Seychelles have symbolic meanings.

Bahamas

Yellow represents the sandy beaches of the Bahamas.

Finland

White represents snow and ice.

Blue represents the sea and sky.

Yellow represents the Sun.

Seychelles

Red represents the people and their determination to work for the future.

White represents social justice and harmony.

Green represents the land.

9

Historic Colours

Some flag colours tell a story about a country's history. In 1785 the King of Spain adopted red and yellow for the national flag. This colour combination was not used by any other nation, so it was easy to distinguish Spain's ships from those of other countries.

Spain

More than 400 years ago Spain controlled the Netherlands. One of the Dutch leaders called Prince William of Orange raised an army to help drive the Spanish out. After winning their freedom, the people of the Netherlands adopted an orange, white and blue flag. This was similar to Prince William's personal flag. Eventually, the orange stripe was changed to red. To this day, the Netherlands' flag honours William's place in the country's history.

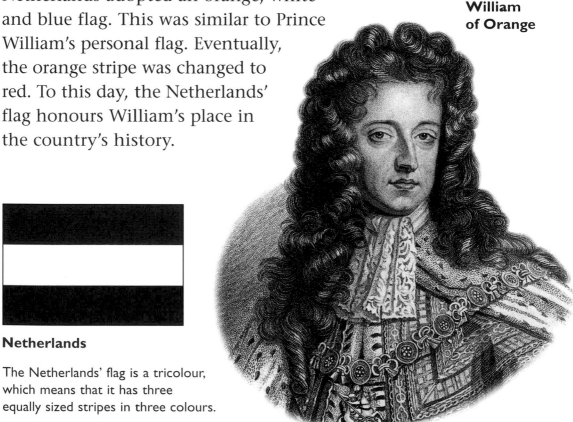

William of Orange

Netherlands

The Netherlands' flag is a tricolour, which means that it has three equally sized stripes in three colours.

Although the French flag is also red, white and blue, the history of this flag is different. White was the colour of the kings of France, while red and blue were the colours of Paris.

During the late 1700s many people in Paris were starving, while the King and members of the ruling class used France's wealth for themselves. In 1792 the people overthrew the King and set up a new government. Since then red, white and blue have represented liberty to people around the world.

France

On 14th July 1789 the French Revolution began when the people of Paris stormed the Bastille prison.

Some nations chose their flag colours or designs because they were inspired by other nations. Peter the Great was an emperor of Russia who lived from 1672 to 1725. He travelled to the Netherlands and took ideas from there back to Russia. He started schools, built a navy and even made people dress differently. Although the two countries used the same colours for their flags, Peter the Great made the horizontal stripes a feature of his own nation's flag.

Paraguay's flag is also red, white and blue. During the nineteenth century, the people of Paraguay fought for independence from Spain. Inspired by the French Revolution, they used the colours of the French flag.

Peter the Great

Russian Federation

Paraguay

Paraguay's flag has the same colours as the French flag. There are different emblems on the front and the back of the flag.

State Arms on front of flag

Treasury Seal on back of flag

Symbols on Flags

Many flags have special symbols that represent important natural features, religious or historic ideas or cultural traditions.

Symbols of Nature

Lebanon has a cedar tree on its flag. This tree is known as the cedar of Lebanon. It has been an important part of Lebanon's history. It provided wood and cedar oil for many ancient civilizations.

Kiribati is an island nation in the Pacific Ocean. It has six wavy bands of blue and white on its flag. These bands represent the ocean waves. The Sun is shown rising from the waves. Above the Sun is a frigate bird.

Lebanon

cedar tree

The frigate bird is found over the Pacific Ocean.

Kiribati

Stars

Many flags have stars on them. Sometimes these stars represent specific stars or constellations. Flags of some countries in the southern hemisphere, including Australia, New Zealand and Papua New Guinea, include a constellation known as the Southern Cross. For centuries sailors in the southern oceans have used this constellation to guide them.

On Cape Verde's flag the ten stars represent the ten main islands that make up the country.

Southern Cross constellation

bird of paradise

Papua New Guinea

Cape Verde

Cape Verde Islands lie in the Atlantic Ocean, off the coast of West Africa.

New Zealand

New Zealand's flag shows the stars of the Southern Cross.

China

Stars represent ideas as well. China's flag has five stars. One star is larger than the others and represents communism. China is ruled by a communist government. The smaller stars represent groups of people in the country, such as workers and peasants.

Guinea-Bissau's flag has a black star. This represents freedom and respect for African people.

A star and crescent Moon are found on flags from many nations where Islam is an important religion such as Malaysia. Other flags have a cross which is a Christian symbol.

Many people in China hang flags from their flats to celebrate Chinese National Day.

Guinea-Bissau

A gold star and crescent Moon are traditional symbols for Muslim people.

Fourteen red and white stripes represent the fourteen states of Malaysia.

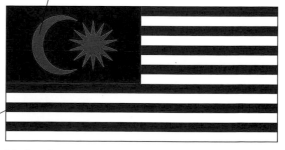

Malaysia

Historic Symbols

Many flags tell the history of a country. Some designs represent an important event such as when a country became independent. Others use symbols from much earlier cultures and times. Argentina's flag does both.

Argentina

In the middle of Argentina's flag is the Sun which celebrates the culture of the Incas, Native Americans of Argentina and other countries of modern-day South America. It represents pride in the Inca culture and also celebrates Argentina's independence from Spain in May 1816.

The Sun of May symbol is part of Argentina's flag.

Early civilizations are represented on other flags, too. Angkor Wat is an ancient temple in Cambodia. It was built almost 1,000 years ago but is still represented on the country's flag.

Cambodia

Angkor Wat is a temple in Cambodia. It is shown on the nation's flag.

Mexico

Arms of Mexico

Mexico's flag has a picture of an eagle sitting on a cactus eating a snake. This picture celebrates an Aztec legend. The Aztecs used to rule Mexico.

Some flags show the traditional weapons of nations of the past. Swaziland's flag has the image of a shield, a staff and two spears. The shield and staff are decorated with the images of feathers from local birds. These symbols represent the fight for independence as well as the traditions of the people of Swaziland.

This Aztec stone carving shows the eagle of Aztec legends.

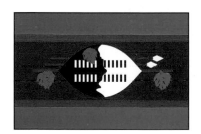

Swaziland

Swazi shields are usually made from cow hides.

Poles are put through rows of slits to make shields rigid.

A symbol representing a yurt is found on the flag of Kyrgyzstan.

Some people in Kyrgyzstan still live in yurts.

Kyrgyzstan

The Sun symbol has forty rays. Each ray represents one of the forty Kyrgyz tribes.

Cultural traditions are also represented on flags. From ancient times, the Kyrgyz (KIR-gihz) people moved from place to place in search of grazing land for their animals. They lived in yurts, or felt tents. Life has changed for most Kyrgyz, but the yurt is still an important part of their culture. It is represented within a yellow Sun symbol on the flag of Kyrgyzstan (kir-gih-STAN).

Turkmenistan's flag has a patterned stripe to represent the tradition of carpet-weaving. Today the people still weave difficult carpet patterns by hand.

Turkmenistan

A stripe on the flag of Turkmenistan represents traditional carpet designs.

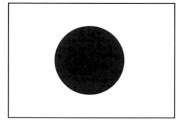

Japan

The Sun rises over Wakayama's rocky coastline in Japan.

Japan's flag is a white rectangle with a red circle in the middle. It celebrates nature, history and religion. *Japan* means "Land of the Rising Sun" and the red circle represents the Sun. The emperor of Japan is believed to be a descendant of a Sun goddess. The red Sun symbol represents this, too.

Circles don't always represent the Sun. On the flag of Bangladesh the red circle represents the blood lost in the country's fight for independence. On Palau's flag the yellow circle represents the Moon and stands for peace. Palau people believe that the full Moon is the best time for harvesting, fishing and celebration.

Bangladesh

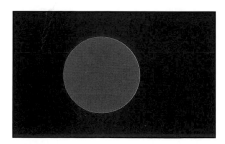

Palau

19

Changing Flags

Nations change over time. Their borders can move because of new agreements between countries or war. Different governments come to power because of new laws or revolution. When nations change, their flags may change, too.

Afghanistan
A new flag was adopted by Afghanistan after the ruling Taliban fell from power in 2001.

The Union Jack

Our flag, the Union Flag, is also known as the Union Jack. It is a combination of the English, Scottish and Irish flags.

In 1603 King James of Scotland became King of England, too. Each country kept its own flag, but the new kingdom flew flags from its ships that combined both designs. In 1801 Ireland became part of the United Kingdom. One of its flags at the time was a red diagonal cross on white. This was added to the United Kingdom's flag. Wales was united with England in the 1500s, but its flag design, which includes a red dragon, is not part of the Union Jack.

United Kingdom
A "jack" is a small flag that is flown on the bow, or front, mast of a ship. In the 1600s an early version of the Union Jack was flown from ships.

The Union Jack and Other Nations

For many centuries the United Kingdom explored the world and set up colonies on different continents. Today most of these colonies are independent nations. Canada, South Africa and India have flags based on traditional designs or symbols that were important before British rule. However, Australia, New Zealand and Fiji continue to include a Union Jack in one corner of their flags.

Canada designed a new national flag in 1965. A red maple leaf was included in the middle white band. This represented the maple tree which has been important to Canadians for hundreds of years. Red and white are the national colours of Canada.

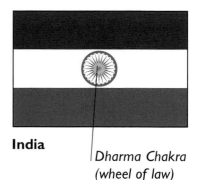

India

Dharma Chakra
(wheel of law)

Fiji

The Union Jack represents
Fiji's historical links with
the United Kingdom.

maple leaf

Canada

Australia has a Union Jack in the top left corner of its flag. Beneath the Union Jack is a seven-pointed star that represents the six states and the territories that make up Australia. The Southern Cross constellation appears on the outer edge of the flag.

Australia

Different groups of people within a country often have their own flag to represent themselves. In Australia the Aboriginal people have their own flag. It is black, gold and red.

Aboriginal flag

Cathy Freeman celebrated an Olympic victory with both the Australian and Aboriginal flags.

The Parts of a Flag

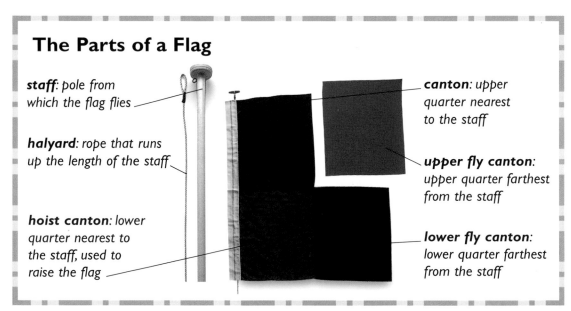

staff: pole from which the flag flies

halyard: rope that runs up the length of the staff

hoist canton: lower quarter nearest to the staff, used to raise the flag

canton: upper quarter nearest to the staff

upper fly canton: upper quarter farthest from the staff

lower fly canton: lower quarter farthest from the staff

The flag of the United States of America used to include a Union Jack. This flag also had thirteen red and white stripes that represented the union of the thirteen original British colonies.

As the American colonies moved towards independence from the United Kingdom, the flag was changed in 1777 to one with thirteen red and white stripes and a blue rectangle with thirteen stars. This was the first version of the Stars and Stripes.

As more states joined the United States, the flag kept changing. At first, a stripe and a star were added for each new state. Later it was decided to keep thirteen stripes, for the original thirteen colonies. Stars were added to show how many states there were. Today there are fifty stars on the flag. The fiftieth star was added in 1960 when Hawaii became part of the United States.

The Union Jack was a symbol of loyalty to the United Kingdom.

Grand Union flag

first Stars and Stripes

Fifty stars represent the number of states in the US today.

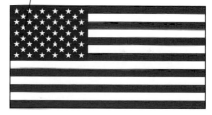

United States

International Flags

Today many countries have come together to form different international organizations. These organizations have flags to identify themselves and their member countries.

Uniting Nations

The United Nations (UN) is an international organization made up of many nations from all around the world. It was set up to keep world peace and to help resolve emergencies and disagreements between nations.

United Nations (UN)

The flag of the United Nations is pale blue which represents peace. It has a white map of the world surrounded by olive branches. These are ancient symbols of peace and harmony.

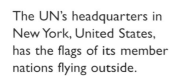

The UN's headquarters in New York, United States, has the flags of its member nations flying outside.

The European Union (EU) is made up of countries in Europe including the United Kingdom, the Republic of Ireland, France, Germany, Spain and Greece. The EU uses the European flag, which is blue with a circle of twelve gold stars. The number of stars has nothing to do with the number of states. In various traditions twelve is a symbolic number representing perfection. The circle is a symbol of unity.

European Union (EU)

The Arab League represents Middle Eastern countries such as Saudi Arabia, Kuwait and Lebanon. A gold chain on the Arab League's flag represents the unity of the countries.

Arab League

The Association of South East Asian Nations (ASEAN) is made up of South East Asian countries such as Singapore, Malaysia and Thailand. Its flag includes ten rice stalks. Each stalk represents one of the ten member nations.

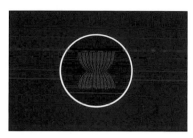

Association of South East Asian Nations (ASEAN)

The Caribbean Community and Common Market (CARICOM) was founded in 1973. Countries that are members include the Bahamas and Jamaica.

Dark blue represents the sea.

Caribbean Community and Common Market (CARICOM)

Light blue represents the sky.

The yellow circle represents the Sun.

The black letters are the initials of the Caribbean Community.

More International Flags

The Red Cross and the Red Crescent flags represent international groups that bring health care and emergency relief to people all over the world. They are symbols of peace and care. Often workers for these organizations are in dangerous locations, including war zones. The flags signal that the workers have no part in the conflict.

Red Crescent

The flag of the Olympic Games displays five interlocking rings representing the union of athletes from five parts of the world – Africa, the Americas, Asia, Australia and Europe.

Red Cross

Some flags have other meanings that are understood worldwide. A plain white flag often means surrender. A yellow flag warns of disease.

Olympic Games

Jolly Roger

A white skull and crossed bones or swords on a black background is the flag of pirate ships.

Flag Customs and Traditions

All over the world people have different customs and traditions in relation to their flags.

This Icelandic flag is flying at half-mast – a sign of respect for an important person who has died.

Respecting the Flag

Citizens of some countries believe that the flag should not be dipped in salute to anyone. It definitely should never touch the ground. However, in other countries dipping a flag is a sign of respect.

In some countries it is disrespectful to write on the flag. Yet in others, it isn't. For example, in Argentina 750 people who gave money to help World War I soldiers signed their names on a decorative Argentinian flag.

During World War II some Japanese soldiers carried national flags into battle with messages written on them.

Flags in Exploration

It is traditional to erect a flag to mark a great event in exploration. Mountaineers, astronauts and adventurers have left their flag at places they have been to.

For example, Roald Amundsen planted the Norwegian flag at the South Pole on 14th December 1911, but this doesn't mean that the South Pole belongs to Norway.

Many countries have flags flying at the South Pole. They represent explorers who have reached the Pole.

There is no wind on the Moon. Flags in space are often specially wired or hung from a horizontal bar to look as though they are fluttering in the breeze.

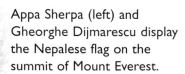

Appa Sherpa (left) and Gheorghe Dijmarescu display the Nepalese flag on the summit of Mount Everest.

Flags and Fun

Flags are flown at festivals all over the world. They also decorate clothes, bags, mugs and plates. Sometimes the whole flag design is printed onto objects, and other times just the colours are used to represent a particular nation.

Flags play a huge role in international sporting events. Spectators cheer on their national team and show support by waving their country's flag.

These Norwegian football fans have painted their faces with the colours of Norway's flag.

At this National Festival of Youth in Burundi, school groups perform traditional dances and songs under their national flag (centre).

North Korea has the tallest supported flagpole in the world. It soars 160 metres into the sky.

Flags of the World

There are more than 190 countries in the world, and all of them have their own national flag. Here you can find the location of the countries whose flags are included in this book.

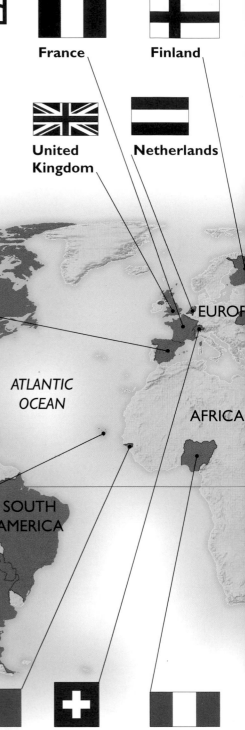

France

Finland

United
Kingdom

Netherlands

Spain

Canada

United States
of America

Mexico

Bahamas

Cape Verde

equator

NORTH
AMERICA

ATLANTIC
OCEAN

EUROPE

AFRICA

PACIFIC
OCEAN

SOUTH
AMERICA

Brazil   Paraguay   Argentina   Guinea-Bissau   Switzerland   Nigeria

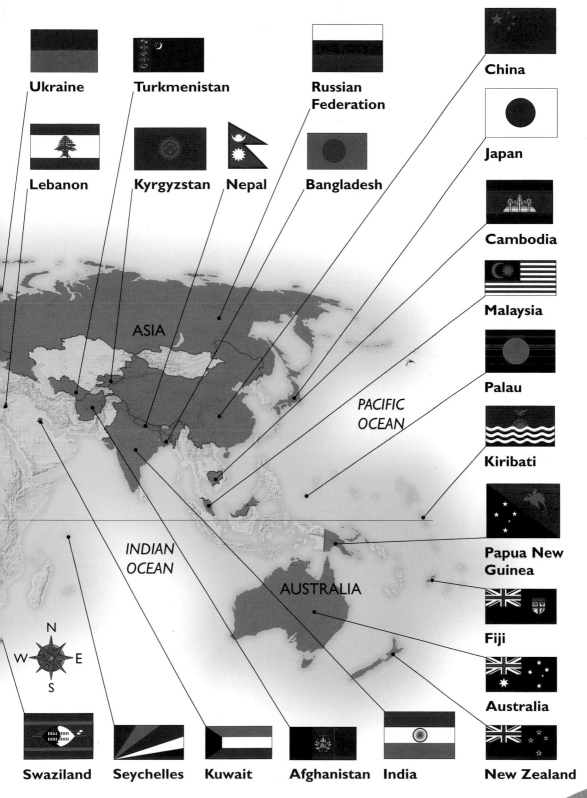

Ukraine

Turkmenistan

Russian
Federation

China

Lebanon

Kyrgyzstan Nepal Bangladesh

Japan

Cambodia

Malaysia

ASIA

Palau

PACIFIC
OCEAN

Kiribati

Papua New
Guinea

INDIAN
OCEAN

AUSTRALIA

Fiji

N

W   E

S

Australia

Swaziland Seychelles Kuwait Afghanistan India New Zealand

Index

Aboriginal flag 22
Amundsen, Roald 28
Arab League 25
Argentina 16, 27
Association of South East Asian
    Nations (ASEAN) 25
Australia 14, 21, 22, 26
Aztec 17
Bahamas 9
Bangladesh 19
Brazil 8
Cambodia 16
Canada 21
Cape Verde 14
China 5, 15
Egypt, ancient 5
European Union (EU) 25
Fiji 21
Finland 9
France 11, 25
Germany 25
Greece 25
Guinea-Bissau 15
Incas 16
India 5, 21
Ireland 20, 25
Islam 15
Japan 19
Kiribati 13
Kuwait 7, 25
Kyrgyzstan 18
Lebanon 13, 25
Malaysia 15, 25
Mexico 17
Middle Ages 6

Nepal 7
Netherlands 10, 12
New Zealand 14, 21
Nigeria 8
Olympic Games 26
Palau 19
Papua New Guinea 14
Paraguay 12
pennants 6
pennons 6
Peter the Great 12
Red Crescent 26
Red Cross 26
Rome, ancient 5
Russia 12
Saudi Arabia 25
Scotland 20
Singapore 25
South Africa 21
South Pole 28
Southern Cross 14, 22
Spain 10, 12, 16, 25
stars 14–15, 22, 23
Swaziland 17
Switzerland 7
Thailand 25
Turkmenistan 18
Ukraine 8
Union Jack 20–23
United Kingdom 20, 21, 25
United Nations (UN) 24
United States of America 23
William of Orange 10
yurts 18